INSTANT POT 3 QUART
COOKBOOK
WITH PICTURES

**Mouthwatering Side Dishes to Elevate
Every Meal with Your 3 Quart Instant Pot**

JOURNEE CRUZ

COPYRIGHT

CHAPTER

TABLE OF CONTENTS

TABLE OF CONTENTS

INTRODUCTION

Introducing "Instant Pot 3 Quart Cookbook With Pictures," a cookbook that combines ease of use with delicious recipes. Published by Journee Cruz, this cookbook is meant to make cooking in an Instant Pot easy and fun.

This cookbook is your go-to guide for making delicious meals in your 3 Quart Instant Pot. It has a carefully chosen collection of mouthwatering recipes accompanied by a variety of bright pictures. Each recipe, from hearty breakfasts to rich desserts, is designed to show off the versatility and efficiency of your Instant Pot while guaranteeing photo-perfect results every time.

Whatever level of experience you have with pressure cooking or the Instant Pot, this book has helpful tips, step-by-step instructions, and expert advice to help you get the most out of your appliance. Desserts, Soups and Stews, Pasta Dishes, Appetizers and Snacks, International Flavors, Vegetarian and Vegan, and Breakfast Recipes, there's something for everyone and every occasion.

Come along on a culinary adventure full of flavour, creativity, and the pure joy of using your Instant Pot to cook. Stop stressing out in the kitchen and start making easy meals that will make your family and guests happy. As you start your tasty journey into the world of pressure cooking, "Instant Pot 3 Quart Cookbook With Pictures" will be your reliable guide.

HOW TO USE INSTANT POT FOR COOKING

The Instant Pot is easy to use and quick to cook with, so it can be used for a lot of different recipes. Here is a simple start-up guide:

Familiarize Yourself with Your Instant Pot: Learn about the parts of your Instant Pot before you start cooking. The control panel, lid, sealing ring, steam release valve, and inner pot are all part of this.

Getting Ready: Get your ingredients ready the way the recipe says to. For example, you could chop up vegetables, measure liquids, and season meats and other foods as needed.

List the ingredients: Add the ready-to-use ingredients to the Instant Pot's inner pot. Make sure you don't fill the inner pot past the line that says "maximum fill."

Secure the lid: Make sure that the sealing ring is in the right place inside the lid, and then put the lid on the Instant Pot securely. Press the lid down by turning it counterclockwise.

Choose the cooking program: Choose the right cooking program from the control panel for your recipe. Settings like Pressure Cook, Slow Cook, Saute, Steam, and more may be available. Change the temperature and cooking time as needed.

Once you've chosen a cooking program and made any necessary changes to the settings, press the "Start" button to start cooking. There will be a delay before the Instant Pot starts cooking while it builds up pressure.

Release of Pressure: There are two main ways to let the pressure out of the Instant Pot after the cooking cycle is over natural release and quick release. To figure out which method to use, read the recipe carefully. Let the pressure slowly go away on its own for a natural release. Remove the pressure quickly by carefully turning the steam release valve to the "Venting" position.

It's okay to open the lid now that the pressure is gone and the float valve has sunk. To open it, carefully turn the lid counterclockwise. Keep the lid away from your face when you open it so the steam doesn't get in.

Take it and enjoy it: Take the inner pot out of the Instant Pot carefully, and then serve your tasty food. Watch out because the inside of the pot and its contents may be hot.

Clean Up: Follow the manufacturer's instructions to clean the Instant Pot parts thoroughly after cooking to keep them working well and lasting a long time.

By following these simple steps, you'll be able to use your Instant Pot to cook a wide range of foods quickly and easily. As you get better at using your Instant Pot, don't be afraid to try out different recipes and ways of cooking to see what works best for you.

TIPS FOR INSTANT POT BEFORE COOKING

Here are some important things you should know before you start cooking with your Instant Pot to make sure you have a safe and successful cooking experience:

Read the Guide:

Read the manual that came with your Instant Pot and get to know it. It has useful details about how to use the appliance properly and safely, along with important guidelines and tips just for your model.

Do the test with water:

You should do a water test before using your Instant Pot for the first time. To do this, you need to put water in the inner pot, close the lid, and run a short pressure cooking cycle. This helps you figure out how the Instant Pot works and makes sure it's working right.

Check the sealing ring:

Ensure the sealing ring (silicone gasket) is in place correctly and free of any damage or dirt. A sealing ring that fits well is necessary to keep the pressure up while cooking.

Check the valve that seals:

This is the steam release valve. Make sure it can move freely and is clean. This is what you should do for proper pressure buildup and release during cooking.

If you need to, preheat:

Heating the Instant Pot up first might be a good idea for some recipes. It is possible to speed up the cooking process by preheating, especially for dishes that need to brown or sauté.

Use the suggested liquid:

Most Instant Pot recipes need a certain amount of liquid to make steam and pressure. As the recipe says, always make sure you have enough liquid, like water, broth, or sauce.

Do not overfill:

Do not put more food in your Instant Pot than the line that says "maximum capacity." This is especially important when cooking foods that expand while cooking, like grains and legumes, or when using the pressure cooking function.

Arrange the ingredients correctly:

As directed in the recipe, layer the ingredients in the inner pot so that the denser ingredients are at the bottom and the lighter ones are on top. This will help the food cook more evenly.

Properly Secure the Lid:

Before you start cooking, ensure the Instant Pot lid is locked securely. Make sure the sealing ring is in the right place and that nothing is blocking a tight seal.

Clear Areas Around It:

Ensure there are no curtains, cabinets, or other appliances blocking the Instant Pot's view while cooking. This will allow air to flow and heat to escape.

If you follow these tips, you'll be better prepared to use your Instant Pot in a safe and effective way, making meals that taste great every time.

INSTANT POT CLEANING PROCESS WITHIN 2 MIN

To keep your Instant Pot working well and lasting long, you need to clean it properly. This is a quick way to clean that only takes two minutes:

Fast Rinse: As soon as you remove the cooked food from the Instant Pot and put it on a serving dish, quickly remove the inner pot from the base and run warm water over it to get rid of any food residue.

Clean Sealing Ring: Take the sealing ring off the lid and wash it in heat soapy water. Make sure you clean both sides of the sealing ring well to get rid of any food or smells that might be stuck inside.

Wipe the lid and base clean:

To get rid of any spills or splatters, quickly wipe down the lid, the area around the sealing ring, and the outside of the Instant Pot base with a damp cloth or sponge.

Dry Parts: Dry the Instant Pot base, sealing ring, lid, and inner pot with a clean dishcloth or towel. Before putting the parts back together, make sure they are all completely dry.

Once everything is dry and clean, put the Instant Pot back together by putting the inner pot back into the base, reattaching the sealing ring to the lid, and locking the lid onto the base. Before you use it again, put the Instant Pot somewhere clean and dry. If you clean your Instant Pot quickly like this, you can keep it in great shape without spending much time on maintenance. You may need to spend more time and use cleaning products like vinegar or baking soda for a deeper clean, especially if there are stains or smells that won't come out.

BREAKFAST

Instant Pot Cinnamon Rolls

 3 servings  25 minutes

Ingredients:

- 0.75 cups of water
- 2.81 ounce tube cinnamon rolls

Instructions:

1. Put water in the bottom of your 6-quart Instant Pot.
2. Spread some butter on a springform pan and put the cinnamon rolls in it. Cover with a paper towel & then foil.
3. Put the pan on a trivet and then put everything in the Instant Pot.
4. Turn off the Keep Warm feature and seal the food. Cook on high pressure for 15 minutes.
5. 10 minutes of slow release, then a quick release
6. To freeze the pan, take it out of the Instant Pot when you're ready to serve. Take off the foil and paper towel.

Peanut Butter Banana Bread

Ingredients:

 3 servings   55 minutes

- 0.13 cups of light brown sugar-packed
- 0.25 tsp vanilla extract
- 0.13 cup of granulated sugar
- 0.17 cup of creamy peanut butter
- 0.25 tsp baking soda
- 0.25 cup of mashed bananas
- 0.06 cup of sour cream
- 0.13 tsp kosher salt
- 0.13 cup of chocolate chips
- 0.25 tsp baking powder
- 0.5 cups of all-purpose flour
- 0.13 cup of unsalted butter
- 0.5 large eggs

Instructions:

1. Spray baking spray on a 7x3-inch springform pan. Put away.
2. Put softened butter, mashed bananas, peanut butter, brown sugar, and granulated sugar in a big bowl. Mix by beating.
3. One at a time, add the eggs and beat well after each one. Put the sour cream and vanilla extract and mix well. Don't forget to clean the bottom and sides of the bowl.
4. Put the baking powder, salt, baking soda, and flour, and mix JUST until everything is mixed. Do NOT over-mix.
5. The chocolate chips should be carefully mixed in.
6. Put the batter into the pan that has been prepared. Use a spatula to level the top. Cover the whole thing with foil.
7. Put 1 and a half cups of water in the Instant Pot's bottom.
8. The pan should be put on a trivet with handles. If your trivet doesn't have handles, you can make a sling out of foil and bring the pan into the pot on top of the trivet.
9. Make sure the valve is set to SEALING, and the lid is locked.
10. Set it to 55 minutes of HIGH PRESSURE. Let the pressure drop naturally for 15 minutes after the cooking time is up.
11. Quickly let go of the pressure that's still there.
12. Take off the pan by opening the lid.
13. The bread should cool in the pan for 10 to 15 minutes. After that, take it out of the pan and set it on a rack to cool.
14. Mix powdered sugar, milk, and vanilla extract for a simple glaze. You can serve the bread as is or wait until it's cool and pour it on top.

Instant Pot Frittata

Ingredients:

 3 servings   6 minutes

- 0.19 cup of crumbled feta cheese
- 0.38 cup of grated Colby cheese
- 0.19 cup of thinly sliced green onion
- 0.09 tsp grated nutmeg
- 0.25 cup of frozen spinach defrosted

- 0.38 tsp salt
- 4.5 large eggs
- 0.75 tbsp grated Parmesan cheese
- 0.25 cup of cream
- 0.09 tsp pepper

Instructions:

1. Spray cooking spray or butter into the wells of a 7x3 oven-safe pan.
2. Put salt and pepper to the eggs and cream, and whisk them together until they are well mixed. Add the cheese, spinach, and onions and mix them in.
3. Put the egg mix into the baking dish that has been prepared. Wrap in foil.
4. Put the cooking rack inside the Instant Pot's inner pot and add two cups of cold water to it. Be careful when you put the baking dish on the cooking rack. Make sure the vent knob is sealed, and close the Instant Pot.
5. Turn the heat up to high and cook for six minutes. (Press by Hand or Pressure) Cook first, then use the +/- buttons to change the time.
6. After the cooking time is up, let the pressure drop naturally for 10 minutes. Then, do a quick release of pressure. Be careful when taking the pan out of the Instant Pot.
7. You can serve it hot or cold.

Instant Pot French Toast Casserole

 3 servings  28 minutes

Ingredients:

- 1 tsp vanilla extract
- 0.5-pound stale brioche challah
- 0.13 cup of brown sugar
- 0.25 tsp salt
- 0.5 + 0.13 cups of whole milk
- 1 tsp ground cinnamon
- 3 large Nellie's Free Range Eggs
- 0.06-0.13 tsp orange zest

Praline Topping:
- 0.06 tsp salt
- 0.17 cup of coarsely chopped pecans
- 1.5 TBSP unsalted butter

- 1 TBSP brown sugar
- 0.13-0.25 tsp ground cinnamon

Vanilla Icing:
- 0.5 cup of powdered sugar
- 1 TBSP unsalted butter
- 1 TBSP cream cheese
- 0.25 tsp vanilla extract

Extras:
- fresh fruit
- Maple syrup for drizzling

Instructions:

1. You will need stale or dried-out bread for this recipe. If you want to make this tasty French toast casserole, you will need to dry out fresh, fluffy bread.
2. Prepare a round baking dish that holds 1.5 quarts and can go in the oven. Spray with cooking spray or rub butter on the inside of the dish to keep things from sticking. No need to: Cut a circle of parchment paper to fit around the dish's bottom. This will make it even easier to take out.
3. In a large bowl, put bread cubes that are 1 inch square. Put away.
4. Add the eggs, milk, brown sugar, vanilla, cinnamon, salt, and orange zest to a medium-sized bowl. If you want a hint of orange flavor, add 1/8 tsp of zest. If you want a big hit of orange flavor, add 1/4 tsp. Mixed with a whisk.
5. For even coverage, pour the egg mix over the cubed bread and mix it in. Pour into the dish that was just prepared.

6. To make the praline topping, which isn't necessary but is sooo good, put the ingredients in a bowl and use your hands to mix them well until the mixture is almost sandy and paste-like. Add to the casserole.

7. Wrap your baking dish in foil to keep moisture out while it's cooking, and set it on top of a trivet with a handle. Foil that has been folded can be used to make your own handle if you only have a regular trivet. My Instant Pot came with one. In the inner pot of the pressure cooker, put one cup of water. Then, put the baking dish on the trivet and lower it into the pot.

8. Set the timer for 28 minutes at high pressure and lock the lid. Make sure the valve is in the closed position.

9. Be sure to make the icing while the casserole is cooking. With your bare hands or a hand mixer, mix softened cream cheese and butter until they are smooth. Add vanilla and powdered sugar, and season with a tiny bit of salt. Add an extra 1/4 tsp of vanilla if you'd like it to taste even better, and mix everything together well.

10. When the Instant Pot beeps, the pressure is quickly released by flipping the valve to the venting position. To take the dish out, use dish towels or gloves to lift it off the trivet by its handle and set it aside. Take off the foil.

11. If you want the topping to be crispy, you can put the casserole in the oven and broil it on HIGH for 3–4 minutes, being careful not to burn or over-toast the bread. You don't have to do this, but if you have a few extra minutes, it gives the texture a great boost. Add icing to the top of the casserole, and then serve it with fresh fruit and maple syrup from the side.

Instant Pot Coffee Cake

 3 servings   20 minutes

Ingredients:

- 0.5 cup of milk
- 0.75 tsp baking powder
- 1.69 cups of all-purpose flour
- 3 tbsp butter
- 0.75 egg
- 0.75 tsp cinnamon
- 0.38 cup of brown sugar

Instructions:

1. To make the streusel, mix together ⅓ cup of brown sugar, ⅓ cup of flour, and cinnamon. With your fingers, work in the butter until big crumbs form.
2. To make the cake, mix the rest of the flour with the sugar, baking powder, milk, melted butter, and baking powder. Mix the batter until it's smooth.
3. Cover an 8-inch spring form pan with some of the streusel. Add some of the batters on top.
4. Cover the batter with the rest of the streusel, then pour the last layer on top.
5. Put the trivet into the Instant Pot and add one cup of water.
6. Put the cake on the platter and cover it with foil.
7. Put the lid back on and set the timer for 20 minutes.
8. Wait for a natural release after the cooking time is up.
9. Take the cake out by opening the lid.
10. Let the cake cool down a bit, then cut it up and serve.

Sausage Gravy

🍴 3 servings   🕐 20 minutes

Ingredients:

- 2 tbsp all-purpose flour
- 2 tbsp butter
- 0.5-pound breakfast sausage mild
- salt & pepper
- 1.25 cups of milk

Instructions:

1. Set the heat to high for saute.
2. Add the sausage to the pot. Cut the sausage into small pieces that you can easily eat. After 5 to 8 minutes, the meat should no longer be pink.
3. Put in the butter and wait for it to melt all the way through.
4. Sprinkle two tbsp of flour on top and mix the meat until it takes up all the flour. Do it again with the last 2 tbsp of flour.
5. Add ½ cup of milk at a time to the flour mixture and stir it all the time. This is important to do so that the gravy doesn't get lumpy.
6. For 8 to 10 minutes, or until it thickens to the consistency you want, stir the gravy often as it cooks. Add pepper and salt to taste. Just add another ½ cup of milk if the gravy gets too thick. Do this again if you need to.

Grits with Cheddar and Jalapeño

 3 servings   🕐 45 minutes

Ingredients:

- 1.13 cups of water
- Salt to taste
- 0.38 cup of heavy cream
- 0.75 Jalapeno peppers
- 0.38 cup of stone ground grits
- 3 ounce sharp cheddar cheese
- 0.75 ounce cream cheese
- 1.5 slices of bacon

Instructions:

1. Put bacon inside. In the Saute menu, choose "Normal" for the heat level. For about 8 minutes, don't touch the bacon while it's cooking on one side. After that, stir your bacon pieces around until they are all cooked. Take it out of the tray and put it on a paper towel to drain.
2. Take out most of the bacon grease from the Instant Pot, leaving about 2 tbsp.
3. To the insert, add the chopped Jalapeno and stir it around for about two minutes, until it gets soft.
4. Stir the grits in for about 10 seconds after adding them.
5. Add some water and use a wooden spoon to scrape up any brown bacon stuck to the pan's bottom. Add salt and heavy cream and mix well.
6. Press the Instant Pot's "Cancel" button. After that, choose "Pressure Cook" and cook for 10 minutes on High Pressure. After it's done, let the pressure in your pressure cooker release naturally for 10 minutes. Then, manually release any pressure that is still there.
7. Add the cheddar cheese and cream cheese after opening the lid.
8. Do not eat the grits until they are cool.
9. Add bacon pieces on top. Enjoy!

Lemon Blueberry Breakfast Cake

Ingredients:

 3 servings   10 minutes

- 3 cups of fresh blueberries
- 1.5 tsp vanilla extract
- 1.5 egg room temp
- 0.75 cup of buttermilk
- 3 tsp baking powder
- 0.75 cup of unsalted butter
- 1.13 cup of sugar
- 0.75 tsp salt
- 3 cups of unbleached all-purpose flour
- 1.5 lemon zest
- 0.75 cup of powdered sugar
- 0.75 lemon juice

Instructions:

1. Grease and flour a dish that is the right size for the Instant Pot.
2. Combine the flour, salt, & baking powder in a small bowl. Set aside 2 tbsp for the next step.
3. Add the zest, sugar, and room-temperature butter to the mixer. While beating, scrape the sides of the bowl as needed to make sure the ingredients are well-mixed.
4. Mix the egg and vanilla in the mixer.
5. Slowly add the flour mix and buttermilk to the softened butter in the stand mixer, one cup of at a time. Mix it all together before adding another cup of, one at a time. Take out the mixer bowl.
6. Toss the blueberries with the flour you saved, and then carefully fold them into the batter.
7. Add two-thirds of a cup of water to the Instant Pot with the rack. Put half of the batter into a dish that has been greased or floured, then move it to the pressure cooker.
8. Timer for 30 minutes on High Pressure in the Instant Pot.
9. When it's done, quickly let go of the pressure and immediately take the cake out. Let the condensation go away completely before moving the food to a serving dish.
10. Pouring half a lemon juice over the cake after mixing it with half a cup of powdered sugar is not required.
11. Serve and have fun!

Breakfast Stuffed Sweet Potatoes

🍴 3 servings   🕐 15 minutes

Ingredients:

- 3 tbsp pure maple syrup
- 3 cups of water
- 3 sweet potato
- 6 tbsp blueberries
- 3 tbsp chopped pecans
- 3 tbsp almond butter
- 3 tsp chia seeds

Instructions:

1. Add the steamer rack and one cup of water to the Instant Pot.
2. On the rack, put the sweet potato. Close the lid and make sure the release valve is in the right place.
3. For 15 minutes, set the Instant Pot to high pressure on its own. It will take a while to get to full pressure.
4. After the time is up, let the pressure go away on its own for ten minutes. To get rid of any extra pressure, turn the release valve. Open the lid and take out the sweet potato once the float valve has dropped.
5. Cut the sweet potato in half and use a fork to mash the flesh once it is cool enough to touch. Put almond butter and maple syrup on top, and then add pecans, blueberries, and chia seeds.

SOUPS AND STEWS

Instant Pot Lentil Soup

 3 servings   10 minutes

Ingredients:

- 0.5 cup of dry green lentils
- 1 garlic cloves, minced
- 0.5 can fire-roasted diced tomatoes
- 0.63 tsp ground cumin
- 0.5 cup of fresh baby spinach
- 0.13 tsp ground black pepper
- 1 celery stalks

- 0.63 tsp curry powder
- 0.5 yellow onion
- 1 carrots
- 2 cups of water
- 0.75 tsp fine sea salt
- fresh parsley & lemon slices
- pinch of cayenne pepper

Instructions:

1. Add the onion, garlic, cumin, curry powder, cayenne (if using), carrots, celery, lentils, salt, pepper, and water to the Instant Pot's stainless steel bowl. Also, add the diced tomatoes and their juices.
2. Put the lid back on and turn the steam valve to the Sealing position. To cook at high pressure for 10 minutes, press the Manual or Pressure Cook button. The pot should reach full pressure in about 15 minutes. Until then, the screen will show "ON."
3. Take out of the oven and let the pressure drop naturally for 10 minutes. Then, open the steam release valve and let the steam out. It's safe to take off the lid when the floating valve falls.
4. To make sure the lentils and vegetables are soft, stir the soup. Then, add the chopped fresh spinach. When the soup gets hot, the greens should quickly wilt. Add more salt if you like, and then serve it warm with lemon slices or chopped fresh parsley on top to make the flavor even better.
5. Soup that you don't want to eat can be kept in the fridge for up to a week in an airtight container.

Instant Pot Vegetable Soup

 3 servings   20 minutes

Ingredients:

- freshly ground black pepper
- 1.5 medium carrots
- 0.75 tsp Red Boat fish sauce
- 2.25 dried shiitake mushrooms
- 1.5 garlic cloves minced
- 1.5 scallions thinly sliced
- Diamond Crystal kosher salt
- 0.75 large shallot
- 4.5 cups of Instant Pot Bone Broth
- 0.75-pound baby bok choy ends

Instructions:

1. Put the broth into the Instant Pot's metal insert.
2. Add the potatoes, carrots, and shallots slowly. Add the garlic, shiitake mushrooms, and Red Boat fish sauce, and mix them in. Be sure to add the baby bok choy.
3. You can lock the lid on top of the Instant Pot and cook on high pressure for two minutes.
4. When the soup is done cooking, manually let go of the pressure. Put salt, fish sauce, and black pepper into the soup based on your taste.
5. Put it in bowls and sprinkle scallions on top.

Instant Pot Minestrone Soup

 3 servings   20 minutes

Ingredients:

- 24 ounces Vegetable Broth
- Parsley
- 1 ½ cups of Spinach
- ¾ can Diced Tomatoes
- ¾ can White Kidney Beans
- ¾ cup of Onion
- ¾ Zucchini
- ¾ tbsp Garlic
- 1 ½ tbsp Olive Oil

- ⅜ cup of Pasta
- 1 ½ Carrot
- 1 ½ Celery Stalks
- ⅕ cup of Parmesan cheese

Seasoning:
- ¾ tsp Salt
- ⅕ tsp Black Pepper
- 1 ½ tsp Italian Seasoning
- ¾ tsp Paprika

Instructions:

1. Set the Instant Pot to SAUTE mode and add olive oil.
2. Cut up some onions and garlic and add them. For two minutes, stir and cook.
3. Chopped celery, carrots, and Zucchini should be added along with diced tomatoes. Add the garlic after adding the salt, pepper, and paprika.
4. The pasta, vegetable broth, and white kidney beans should all be added now. Mix everything together. Make sure the pasta is below the water.
5. Press "Cancel," then close the lid with the vent in the "sealing" position. Turn it on to the SOUP setting and leave it there for 5 minutes.
6. Wait five minutes after the instant pot beeps for the pressure to release on its own. Then, let go of the pressure by hand.
7. Take a five-minute break, and then add the chopped Spinach.
8. Add Parmesan cheese if you want, and the minestrone soup is ready to be served.

Broccoli and Cheese Soup

Ingredients:

🍴 3 servings 🕐 30 minutes

- 1.2 cloves garlic
- 0.6 cup of matchstick carrots
- 0.08 tsp red pepper flakes
- 0.15 cup of cold water
- 1.2 tbsp butter
- 0.15 tsp salt
- 0.6 cup of diced Onion
- 1.2 cups of grated cheddar cheese
- 2.4 cups of bite-sized broccoli florets
- 2.4 cups of vegetable broth
- 0.15 tsp ground black pepper
- 1.2 cups of cream or half-and-half
- 0.15 cup of corn starch

Instructions:

1. To heat up the pressure cooker, choose "browning/saute." After adding the Onion and butter, it will take about 3 minutes to cook.
2. The garlic should smell good after about 30 seconds of cooking.
3. Salt, pepper, red pepper flakes, broccoli, and chicken stock should all be mixed in.
4. Lock the lid in place and make sure the vent is set to close. Then, choose high pressure and a one-minute cooking time.
5. Press the "quick release" button when the cooking time is up. Be careful when taking off the lid after the valve drops.
6. Mix the cornstarch and cold water in a small bowl with a whisk until the mixture is smooth.
7. Put the pressure cooker on "saute" or "browning," and slowly put the corn starch mixture into the pot. Keep stirring the soup until it boils and gets thick.
8. After using it, turn it off. Add the cream or half-and-half slowly while stirring.
9. Slowly add the cheese and mix it in until it melts.
10. Put more pepper and salt to taste, and serve hot.

Instant Pot Potato Soup

Ingredients:

3 servings   8 minutes

- 3.75 Pounds Russet Potatoes
- 1.5 Tbsp Cornstarch
- 0.75 Tsp Garlic Powder
- 0.75 Tsp Onion Powder
- 0.38 Tsp Salt
- 3.75-4.5 Cups of Chicken Broth
- 0.38 Tsp Pepper
- 1.5 Cups of Shredded Cheese
- 0.75 Pound Package Cubed Ham
- 0.38 Cup of Milk
- 0.38 Cup of Sour Cream
- 1.5 Tbsp Cold Water
- Green Onions and Extra Cheese

Instructions:

1. Put your cubed and peeled potatoes in the bottom of your instant pot.
2. Pepper, salt, onion powder, ham, and chicken broth should all be added.
3. Put the lid on top of the instant pot and tighten it.
4. Just set the Instant Pot to "Manual" and wait 8 minutes.
5. After the timer goes off, quickly let go and carefully take off the lid.
6. Put the sour cream and milk into the soup and mix them together.
7. The cornstarch and water should be mixed together in a small bowl.
8. Add the cornstarch and water mixture in a saute mode and stir it in with a whisk until the soup gets thick.
9. Take the pot from the heat and stir in the cheese until it melts.
10. Add green onions and extra cheese on top if you want.

Potato Leek Soup

Ingredients:

 3 servings   🕓 6 minutes

- 0.6 cup of canned coconut milk
- 0.45 tsp dried thyme
- 1.8 medium leeks
- 1.2 bay leaves
- 1.2 tbsp grapeseed oil
- 2.4 cups of vegetable broth
- 0.3 tsp ground coriander
- 0.3 tsp dried rosemary
- 0.6 small onion, diced
- 3 small russet potatoes
- Fresh ground pepper
- 1.8-2.4 cloves garlic
- 0.6 tsp salt

Instructions:

1. Put the oil in the Instant Pot and set it to "saute." Add the onions and leeks when the pan is hot. For about 4 to 6 minutes, until softened, saute.
2. Place the coriander, thyme, rosemary, and garlic in the pan. In about 30 to 60 seconds, the food will smell good.
3. Stop the saute function. Put in the potatoes, vegetable broth, bay leaf, salt, and pepper now. Put the lid on and close it. Move the handle to let steam out to the "Sealing" position. Press the "Manual Setting" button on the pressure cooker to turn it on to high pressure. Use the "+" or "-" buttons to set the time for 6 minutes.
4. It will sound an alarm when the time is up. Carefully move the handle that lets out steam to the Venting position. A lot of steam and water will come out in a loud burst. You can open the lid when the Float Valve goes down.
5. Take out the bay leaves and add the coconut milk (start with the shake can). Use a regular blender to blend until the mixture is smooth and creamy. If you think it needs it, put more salt & pepper. If the soup is too thick for your taste, you can add some vegetable broth for ideas on how to top it.

Instant Pot Butternut Squash Soup

 3 servings   10 minutes

Ingredients:

- 0.75 tbsp curry powder
- 1.13 tsp fine sea salt
- 1.5 garlic cloves
- 0.75 large yellow onion
- 0.75 tbsp extra-virgin olive oil
- 1.5 pounds butternut squash
- 2.25 cups of water
- 0.38 cup of canned coconut milk

Instructions:

1. Press the Instant Pot's Saute button and wait one minute for the bottom to warm up. Put in the onion and olive oil. Cook for 5 to 8 minutes, until the Onion gets soft. Then, add the curry powder and garlic. Stir for one more minute until they start to smell good. Press the "Off/Cancel" button and add one cup of water to help keep the garlic from getting too hot. Utilize a wooden spoon or spatula to clear out the pot's bottom. Once the time is up, turn the steam release valve to venting to let out any extra pressure. It's safe to take off the lid once the floating valve has sunk. Put the soup in a blender and blend it slowly until it's smooth. To keep everyone safe, take out the blender's lid vent and cover it with a thin towel to let steam escape. So the steam pressure won't push the lid off your blender. You can work on the soup in batches or use an immersion blender to blend it in the pot. After putting the coconut milk back in the pot, stir the coconut milk into the soup. Taste it and add more salt if needed. You can also put a little maple syrup if the soup tastes sweeter. Warm it up and top it with whatever you want. You can sprinkle extra coconut milk on top or add roasted butternut squash seeds, fresh cilantro, or black pepper. Leftovers can be kept in the fridge for up to five days in a container without air.

Chicken Noodle Soup

Ingredients:

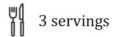 3 servings    25 minutes

- 1.5 cups of water
- 0.38 tsp salt
- 0.38 tsp thyme
- 1.88-ounce egg noodles
- 0.38 large onion
- 1.5 cups of chicken broth
- 0.38 tsp pepper
- 0.75 pounds chicken

- 0.38 tbsp oregano
- 0.75 tbsp butter
- 0.38 chicken bouillon
- 0.38 tbsp parsley
- 0.75 medium carrots
- 0.75 stalks celery

Instructions:

1. Set your Instant Pot to saute.
2. Put in the butter and cook it until it melts. Put in the Onion, carrots, and celery. Saute for three minutes until the Onion gets soft and clear.
3. Put in some pepper and salt, then the thyme, parsley, oregano, and chicken bouillon. Give it a stir.
4. Add the chicken broth. Put in the chicken pieces and four more cups of water.
5. Close the lid. Look at the manufacturer's guide to learn how to close the instant pot lid. Pick the "Soup" setting on the Instant Pot and set the timer for 7 minutes. It's okay if your Instant Pot doesn't have a Soup setting. Just set it to Manual and wait 7 minutes.
6. Wait until the natural release cycle is over after the Instant Pot cycle is done. This should take about 10 minutes. If you're in a hurry, follow the maker's instructions for quick release. Carefully open the instant pot's lid and take it off.
7. Take the chicken out of the soup and use two forks to shred it.
8. Set the Instant Pot back to the saute setting and add the noodles to the soup. Leave the lid off and cook for another 6 minutes or until the noodles are done.
9. Turn off the Instant Pot. Put the chicken shreds back into the Instant Pot. Check the seasoning and make any necessary changes. If you want, you can add more parsley as a garnish.

PASTA DISHES

Creamy Tuscan Chicken Pasta

 3 servings   🕐 30 minutes

Ingredients:

- 6 ounce uncooked campanelle pasta
- 0.5 carton low-sodium chicken broth
- 0.5-pound chicken breasts
- 0.5 cups of parmesan cheese
- 2.5 ounce fresh baby spinach
- 1 tsp Italian seasoning
- 0.5 pkg. Light cream cheese
- 0.5 Tbsp garlic
- 0.13 cup of chopped fresh basil
- Salt and freshly ground black pepper
- 0.25 cups of oil-packed sun-dried tomatoes with herbs

Instructions:

1. Add broth, tomatoes, Italian seasoning, garlic, 1/4 tsp salt, and 1/4 tsp pepper to an Instant Pot insert. Stir to combine. If you need more seasoning, add it at the end.
2. Add the chicken and pasta, and try to mix them into the broth.
3. Hold the lid in place and make sure the pressure valve is in the "sealing" position. Pick "manual" or "high pressure" and set the timer for 5 minutes.
4. Select "Cancel" when the time is up, and then use the "quick release" method to let the pressure go. To do this, carefully turn the valve to the "venting" position and step back as the steam comes out.
5. Once it stops sputtering, remove the lid and stir the noodles immediately to separate them. Then add the Spinach, light cream cheese, and Parmesan.
6. Throw well. It will initially look like soup, but it will get thicker as it rests and cools. Give it 5 to 10 minutes.
7. Add the basil right before serving, and serve it warm. If you want, you can decorate it with some diced sun-dried tomatoes.
8. The recipe was taken from Betty Crocker and changed a bit.

Shrimp Pasta with Vodka Sauce

🍴 3 servings 🕐 6 minutes

Ingredients:

- 8 ounces large raw shrimp
- 0.25 cup of chopped Onion
- 2 cloves garlic
- 1.5 cups of water
- 8 ounces dried penne pasta
- Salt and pepper
- 14 ounces crushed tomatoes
- 0.5 tbsp butter
- 0.13-0.25 tsp crushed red pepper
- 0.25 cup of vodka
- 0.25 cup of heavy cream
- Garnish: Parmesan cheese

Instructions:

1. You can set the pressure cooker to Saute. Break up the red pepper and add it to the pan with the butter. To soften the onions, saute them for three to five minutes, stirring every now and then.
2. Crush the tomatoes and mix them with the water, vodka, penne, and 3/4 tsp of salt. Toss the pasta to coat it.
3. Put the lid on top and lock it in place. Press "High" on the Instant Pot and wait 4 minutes. After cooking the food, turn off the Instant Pot and press the Quick Release button until the valve button falls.
4. Take the lid off and mix the shrimp and cream into the pasta. The Instant Pot should be set to Saute. Cook the shrimp for two to three minutes until they turn pink. If you think it needs it, put salt and pepper. If you want, serve it warm with Parmesan cheese.

Creamy Garlic Chicken Pasta

 3 servings  5 minutes

Ingredients:

- 0.38-pound chicken breast
- 0.38 red bell pepper
- 0.38-pound fettuccine pasta broke
- 0.38 tsp dried oregano
- 0.38 medium onion
- 0.28 cup of freshly grated Parmesan cheese
- 1.31 cups of chicken broth

- 0.38 Tbsp Italian seasoning
- 0.19 cup of heavy cream
- salt and pepper
- 1.5 cloves garlic
- 0.75 Tbsp olive oil
- 0.56 cups of chopped fresh Spinach (optional)
- Optional garnish: freshly chopped flat-leaf parsley and more grated Parmesan

Instructions:

1. Put the Instant Pot in "saute" mode. Add salt and pepper to the chicken.
2. Put the olive oil in the hot pot and wait one minute for it to warm up. After that, add the chicken. Both sides of the chicken should be browned. This may need to be done in groups.
3. Put the onions and bell pepper in after the meat has browned and cook for one more minute.
4. Get rid of the saute setting.
5. The garlic, Italian seasoning, oregano, and fettuccine should then be added. Make the fettuccine spread out so that it cooks on all sides. Place the fettuccine in a bowl and add the chicken broth.
6. Press the seal button on the valve (if your instant pot has one), and then close the pot.
7. Set the pressure to "high" and cook for 5 minutes. It might take ten minutes for it to get really hot.
8. Once you're done, quickly let the pressure go by turning the valve to the vent position. It might take a few minutes for the pressure to go away completely.
9. Start up the Instant Pot. After stirring everything, put the heavy cream, Spinach, & Parmesan cheese.
10. Add the lid back on the Instant Pot and wait a few minutes. This will help the cheese melt, and the Spinach gets soft.
11. Add salt and pepper to taste after opening the Instant Pot and mixing it well.
12. Then you should serve. Some of the sauce will still fall to the bottom of the pot even after you stir it. Spread some of that sauce over the fettuccine that has been served. Add more freshly grated Parmesan cheese and chopped parsley on top if you want.

Instant Pot Bruschetta Chicken Pasta

🍴 3 servings   🕐 15 minutes

Ingredients:

- 0.5 cup of parmesan cheese
- 0.5 tbsp olive oil
- 1 cloves garlic
- 1 medium-sized chicken breast
- 1 cups of water
- 0.5-pound rotini pasta
- 0.5 can diced tomatoes

Bruschetta:
- 0.5 small red onion
- 1 cloves garlic minced
- 0.25 cup of fresh basil
- 2.5 plum tomatoes
- 0.5 tbsp olive oil
- 0.25 each tsp Salt and pepper

Instructions:

1. This is the order in which to add the chicken, garlic, olive oil, water, diced tomatoes, and rotini to the Instant Pot. For three minutes, cook at high Pressure. After that, the Pressure is quickly released. It will take the Instant Pot about 10 to 15 minutes to heat up. After that, it will cook for 3 minutes.
2. In the meantime, make your own bruschetta by combining all the ingredients listed under "bruschetta."
3. Open the Instant Pot's lid when it's safe to do so, and the Pressure has gone out. Add the bruschetta and Parmesan cheese and mix them in well.
4. Put some extra fresh basil on top, serve, and enjoy!

Instant Pot Pasta Carbonara

Ingredients:

🍴 3 servings   🕐 15 minutes

- 0.75 tbsp olive oil
- 1.5 tbsp butter divided
- 0.75 large egg
- 0.19 tsp black pepper
- 4.5 slices of bacon
- 6 ounce. spaghetti noodles
- 0.56 cup of shredded Parmesan cheese
- 1.5 garlic cloves
- 3.38 cups of water

Instructions:

1. Take a handful of spaghetti noodles at a time, split them in half, and arrange them in a cross shape. Put water in. Don't stir. Add some butter to the pasta. Put the lid on. Put the valve in the "sealing" position. Make sure that HIGH Pressure is selected in the IP. Set the timer for 7 minutes and press the "manual" button. There is a 10-minute window for the IP to reach Pressure.

2. Press the "cancel/off" button when the timer is up. After one minute, turn the valve to the "venting" position to let the Pressure out. After the pin falls and the Pressure is gone, carefully open the lid away from your face. Take out ½ cup of the pasta water and set it aside. Put the pasta in a colander and drain it. Throw away any extra pasta water. Keep the spaghetti in the colander.

3. In the Instant Pot, put the insert back in. Choose the "saute" setting. Wait one minute. Fill it with olive oil. Put in the bacon and cook it until it gets crispy. First, add the garlic. Then, cook the bacon for one minute. Put in a tbsp of butter and let it melt. The "cancel/off" button should be pressed. Put the pasta back in the IP. Put bacon, garlic, and grease on top and toss well.

4. Mix the egg and Parmesan in a small bowl. Add the egg and Parmesan mixture slowly while stirring all the time to keep the egg from scrambling. It should turn into a smooth sauce. Add the pasta water you saved and stir well, a little at a time. It should be creamy to eat.

5. Add black pepper. Add more grated Parmesan and chopped parsley on top before serving.

Creamy Garlic Parmesan Pasta

Ingredients:

🍴 3 servings 🕐 8 minutes

- 1 cup of heavy whipping cream
- 3 dashes of ground black pepper
- 1 tsp salt
- 1/4 cup of shredded Parmesan cheese
- 2 1/4 cups of chicken broth
- 2 tbsp lemon juice
- 1 tsp garlic powder
- 2 tbsp olive oil
- 3 cloves garlic
- 8-ounce linguine
- 1 tbsp chopped Italian parsley

Instructions:

1. Long pieces of linguine should be broken in half.
2. Add the olive oil and set the Instant Pot to Saute mode. Once the oil is hot, put the garlic and cook for 10 seconds. Put in the linguine, chicken broth, garlic powder, lemon juice, salt, and black pepper.

IMPORTANT:

1. Be sure to stir the linguine to the sides of the Instant Pot and cover them with liquid.
2. Choose Manual and set the Pressure to High for 8 minutes. Then, cover the pot. Press the Quick Release button when it beeps.
3. As soon as the valve drops, carefully take off the lid. Add heavy cream, Parmesan cheese, and chopped parsley to stir the pasta. If the sauce is too thin, put the pan on "Saute" mode for about one minute to thin it out. Serve right away. You can add more Parmesan cheese and/or lemon wedges on top.

Instant Pot Penne Pasta

Ingredients:

 3 servings   5 minutes

- 0.75 sweet onion
- 6 ounces of dried penne
- 0.75 tbsp Italian Seasoning Spice Blend
- 0.75 cup of diced zucchini
- 0.19 tsp Sea Salt
- 0.75 tbsp balsamic vinegar
- 0.75 can of Diced Tomatoes
- 0.75 cup of bell pepper chopped
- 0.19 tsp Crushed Red Pepper Flakes
- 2.25 cloves minced garlic
- 1.5 tbsp olive oil
- 2.25 tbsp tomato paste
- 1.5 cups of Vegetable Stock

Instructions:

1. Put your Instant Pot in Saute Mode. Put in the zucchini, bell pepper, onions, garlic, and olive oil. For six to seven minutes, or until the vegetables start to get soft, saute them.
2. Add the tomatoes, tomato paste, and balsamic vinegar, and mix well with the Italian spices.
3. Put the pasta in the Instant Pot. Add the vegetable stock to the pasta and mix it well. Don't stir. Put the lid on and lock it. Bring it to a boil.
4. Take care not to put your face or hands near the steam valve as you quickly let the steam out.
5. Stir the pasta after the steam has left and the pressure valve has gone down. For a few minutes more, it will keep getting thicker.
6. Put fresh garlic bread on the side and add parmesan cheese on top if you want. Enjoy!

Philly Cheesesteak Pasta

🍴 3 servings   🕐 15 minutes

Ingredients:

- 3.75 ounces mozzarella cheese
- 0.38 large yellow onion
- 0.19 tsp salt
- 0.75 tbsp butter
- 1.13 tbsp Worcestershire sauce
- 0.56 tsp black pepper
- 0.38-pound ground beef
- 0.19 tsp chili powder
- 0.75 tbsp ketchup
- 0.75 cloves garlic
- 1.13 cups of beef broth
- 0.38 pound rigatoni pasta
- 0.38 large green bell pepper

Instructions:

1. Add the Instant Pot to saute and melt the butter. Turn on the heat and add the garlic.
2. Put in the diced onions and green peppers. Cook for one to two minutes to make the vegetables soft.
3. When you add the ground beef, cook it until it's all browned. Three to four minutes. Use a spoon to take off any extra grease.
4. After turning off the Instant Pot, add salt, pepper, ketchup, chili powder, Worcestershire sauce, and beef broth. Mix everything together well.
5. Put in the rigatoni and mix it in with the ground beef.
6. Add the lid on top of the Instant Pot and set the valve to "seal." Press "high pressure" to cook under high Pressure. For three minutes, set the timer. The pasta will be just right when it's al dente. Add one minute to the cooking time if you want the pasta to be softer.
7. When the pasta is done, let the Pressure out, turn off the Instant Pot, and open the valve. When you take off the lid, slowly stir in the mozzarella cheese. Make sure that everything is well mixed.
8. Serve right away and top with chopped fresh parsley. Enjoy!

Instant Pot Refried Beans

Ingredients:

 3 servings   🕐 40 minutes

- ¼ tsp cayenne
- 1 tsp oregano
- 1 tsp chili powder
- 2 cups of vegetable broth
- 1 cup of dried pinto beans
- ¾ tsp salt
- 1 tbsp olive oil
- 1 tsp cumin
- ½ medium onion
- 2-2 ½ cloves garlic
- ½ tsp paprika

Instructions:

1. Soak the beans in clean water for at least 8 hours or overnight. Before you use them, drain and rinse them again.
2. Put the beans, broth (or water), oil, minced garlic, chopped onion, and all the spices into the Instant Pot. Stir it up.
3. Put the lid back on and set the pressure cooker to Bean/Chili or Pressure. Set the timer for 30 minutes and cook. Once that's done, wait 10 minutes for the Pressure to drop naturally, and then release the Pressure by hand. When the pin hits the bottom, open the lid.
4. Use a potato masher to break up the beans until they are the consistency you want. You can also use a hand blender and blend it a few times, each time for two to three seconds. For a few minutes, or until the beans reach the thickness you want, turn on Saute and let them cook.
5. They taste great with tortillas, tostadas, or as a dip for chips. Top them with chopped cilantro and cheese.

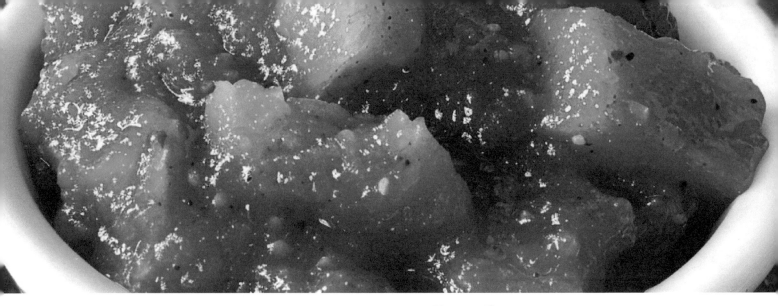

Instant Pot Peach Chutney

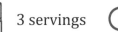 3 servings  15 minutes

Ingredients:

- ⅜ tsp cumin seeds
- ⅜ tsp cayenne pepper
- ⅛ cup of Apple Cider vinegar
- Salt per taste
- 4/7 inch ginger
- 1 ½ cups of chopped ripe

Instructions:

1. Clean and dry the peaches. Take out the pit and cut them up.

Instant Pot Directions:

1. Start up the Instant Pot. Salt, spices, vinegar, and peaches should all be added. Put in ⅓ cup of water. Press or Manually Set After cooking for two minutes, let the Pressure go away on its own for ten minutes. After that, you can move the seal to the Vent to let out any extra pressure.
2. Open the lid and set the heat to high. Stir it about every two to three minutes. If the chutney has thinned out to the consistency of jam, it's done. Stop the Saute. Then, serve it when it's cool enough to touch. Keep the peach chutney in the fridge. The food should last a few weeks! I keep it in the freezer for up to three months.

Instant Pot Caponata

 3 servings  10 minutes

Ingredients:

- 0.75 zucchini
- 0.38 eggplant
- 0.38 tsp salt
- 0.38 pound Roma tomatoes
- 0.38 onion
- 0.38 tbsp brown sugar
- 0.19 cup of tomato paste
- 0.09 tsp black pepper
- 0.09 cup of dates
- 0.19 cup of chopped parsley
- 0.75 tbsp red wine vinegar
- 1.13 celery stalks

Instructions:

1. Put everything into the pressure cooker except for the ¼ cup of tomato paste.
2. Set the timer for 5 minutes.
3. After the quick release, add the last ¼ cup of tomato paste and mix it in. Put it out with different kinds of crackers, flatbread, pita bread, and olives. There are two ways to eat this sauce: hot or cold. It goes well with both pasta and couscous.

Buffalo Chicken Bites

 3 servings   11 minutes

Ingredients:

- 0.19 cup of Franks Red Hot Sauce
- 0.75 pounds of chicken breast
- 0.38 tsp cayenne pepper
- 0.38 tsp black pepper
- 0.09 cup of Franks Red Hot Sauce

Instructions:

1. Cut your chicken into strips that are easy to eat. 0.75 pounds of chicken breast
2. Add the Instant Pot to saute and melt the butter. Add the chicken and seasonings after the butter has melted. After that, add ½ cup of Frank's Hot Sauce and mix it well. 0.38 tsp black pepper, 0.38 tsp cayenne pepper, and 0.19 cup of Frank's Red Hot Sauce
3. Put the lid on your pot and lock it. Then, set it to Pressure. Use high Pressure to cook. For 8 minutes, set the timer.
4. Take the chicken out of the pot. Spread the rest of the hot sauce on top and eat it right away, or put it on a baking sheet and broil it. 0.09 cups of Frank's Red Hot Sauce
5. No need to: With tongs, take the chicken out of the Instant Pot and put it on a baking sheet that has been lined with aluminum foil. Use the extra 1/4 cup of hot sauce to brush on the chicken. Put the chicken under the broiler for 3 minutes to brown it and make the sauce thicker. Do it again on the other side of the chicken after flipping it over. Before you serve the chicken, let it cool for 5 minutes.

Cilantro Lime Chicken Drumsticks

🍴 3 servings 🕐 15 minutes

Ingredients:

- 4 cloves minced garlic
- 1 tsp crushed red peppers
- 1/2 cup of chicken broth
- 1 tbsp olive oil
- 6 drumsticks
- 2 tbsp chopped cilantro
- juice from 1 lime
- 1 tsp cayenne pepper

Instructions:

Instant Pot Instructions:

1. In the Instant Pot, press "Saute" and put the olive oil. Put the chicken drumsticks in the oil once it's hot. Season the drumsticks with the cayenne pepper, minced garlic, and crushed red pepper.
2. Put the chicken stock, cilantro, and lime juice in the Instant Pot. The pressure valve should be set to seal, and the lid should be locked in place.
3. Put the food through 9 minutes of high Pressure.
4. Let the pressure drop on its own when the cooking time is up.
5. Place the drumsticks on a baking sheet and broil for three to five minutes or until they are golden brown. Add fresh cilantro on top, and serve while still warm.

Jalapeno Popper Chicken Dip

 3 servings   🕐 15 minutes

Ingredients:

- ¼ cup of water
- ⅗ cups of shredded mozzarella cheese
- ⅗ large jalapeno peppers
- cooked, crumbled bacon
- 2 ⅖ ounces cream cheese
- ⅐ cup of sour cream
- ⅗ tsp dried minced onions
- ⅓ tsp sea salt
- ½ pounds chicken breasts
- ⅓ tsp garlic powder
- ⅓ cup of shredded cheddar cheese

Instructions:

1. Add minced onions, sea salt, and garlic powder to the chicken in the Instant Pot.
2. Sprinkle about half of the diced Jalapeno peppers on top. Save some for the topping later.
3. Put the lid on, set the vent to "Sealing," and press "CEO" to cook for 10 minutes. Let the pressure release naturally for 10 minutes after the cooking time is up, then do a quick release. Open the lid and shred the chicken with a hand mixer when the pin falls.
4. Add the cream cheese little by little and mix it in until it's well mixed in. Put the sour cream and mix it in well.
5. Put the chicken in a casserole dish and add 1 cup of mozzarella cheese. Add the rest of the cheddar cheese, mozzarella cheese, and diced jalapenos on top. If you want, add crumbled bacon.
6. At 400 degrees, bake until the dip is bubbling and the cheese melts. Serve right away

Instant Pot Chicken Wings

🍴 3 servings   🕐 20 minutes

Ingredients:

- 0.38 tsp paprika
- 3 pounds of chicken wings
- 0.75 tsp thyme
- 0.75 tsp oregano
- 0.19 tsp cayenne
- 0.75 cup of BBQ sauce
- 0.38 tsp garlic powder
- 0.75 tsp salt
- 0.38 tsp black pepper
- 0.38 tsp onion powder

Instructions:

1. Two pounds of chicken wings should be rinsed and dried with paper towels. Add the seasoning and mix it in well until it's all covered.
2. Put the trivet in the Pressure Cooker and add one cup of water.
3. Put the meat that has been seasoned on top of the trivet.
4. Put the lid on top of the pot and set the pressure to high for 6 minutes.
5. After you're done, let the pressure drop on its own for 10 minutes.
6. Then, put the wings in a big bowl and add ½ cup of BBQ sauce. Be sure to mix the wings well.
7. Place the chicken wings on a wire rack-lined baking sheet. If you still have some BBQ sauce in the bowl, use a baking brush to cover the wings with it.
8. Put it under the broiler for 5 to 10 minutes or until the skin is charred and crispy.

Instant Pot Buffalo Chicken Dip

 3 servings 10 minutes

Ingredients:

- ⅐ cup of shredded mozzarella cheese
- ⅓ tbsp water
- ½ large chicken breasts
- ⅐ cup of shredded cheddar cheese
- ⅐ 8-ounce package of cream cheese
- ⅐ 12-ounce bottle of hot wing sauce
- ⅛ cup of ranch dressing
- ½ tbsp butter

Instructions:

1. Cover the chicken breasts with water and hot sauce in the Instant Pot. Put butter on top of the chicken, but don't stir it. Put the lid on top, open the vent all the way, and press "Pressure Cook" for 10 minutes.
2. The pot will be pressurized for a few minutes. After that, it will cook for ten minutes. Either do a quick release or let it naturally release for 10 minutes. Then, do a quick release.
3. Put the lid on and add the cream cheese and ranch dressing. When the pin drops, shred the chicken with a hand mixer until everything is well mixed. Or, take the chicken out of the pot and shred it with forks. Then, put the chicken back in the pot and mix in the ranch and cream cheese until everything is well combined and creamy. If you want a thicker dip, you can take out some of the cooking liquid.
4. Put chicken dip in a casserole dish that can go in the oven. Top with shredded cheese. Ten minutes at 400 degrees or until the dip starts to bubble.

Instant Pot Chicken tacos

 3 servings    20 minutes

Ingredients:

- 1/2 cup of chicken broth
- 1.5 pounds boneless skinless chicken breasts
- 1 cup of salsa
- 2 tbsp taco seasoning
- 1 tbsp olive oil

For Serving:

- Pico de gallo
- Cilantro
- Tortillas or taco shells
- Sour Cream
- Shredded cheese
- Avocado

Instructions:

1. When you put the salsa, chicken broth, taco seasoning, and oil in the instant pot, stir it to mix. Set the Instant Pot to high pressure and add the chicken breasts. Cook for 15 minutes.
2. Use the "quick release" button to let go of the pressure when the time is up. You can also let it go on its own if you want to. Fork-shred the chicken or use an electric mixer to do it. Then mix it all together.

SIDE DISHES

Instant Pot Applesauce

 3 servings   15 minutes

Ingredients:

- 0.25 cup of water
- 0.5 tbsp freshly squeezed lemon juice
- 0.25 tsp ground pumpkin pie spice
- 0.75 pounds of sweet apples
- 0.75 pounds tart apples

Instructions:

1. Peel and core the apples to get them ready. Put the pieces that are about an inch thick in the bottom of a 6-quart Instant Pot.
2. Simply add the water, lemon juice, and pumpkin pie spice (or cinnamon).
3. Protect the Instant Pot by closing the lid. After 8 minutes of cooking on HIGH/Manual pressure, vent to let out the rest of the pressure. It's okay if you forget to do this right away.
4. Mash the applesauce with a wooden spoon or a potato masher.
5. You can use an immersion blender to make it smoother or switch to a regular blender and puree it in batches. Taste and add sweetener. Add an extra 1/4-1/2 tsp of pumpkin pie spice or cinnamon if you want it spicier. Feel free to eat it hot, cold, or room temperature.

Instant Pot Cranberry Sauce

 3 servings   10 minutes

Ingredients:

- ⅛ cup of agave syrup
- 2 4/7 ounces fresh cranberries
- ⅛ cup of water or orange Juice
- ⅕ pinch salt
- ⅕ tsp zest of 1 orange optional

Add After Pressure Cooking:

- ⅛ cup of sugar

Instructions:

1. Turn on the Instant Pot and plug it in. Add orange juice or water first, then maple syrup (or agave). By pouring water on top, you can keep the syrup from burning and sticking to the bottom.
2. Put in the salt and cranberries. Close the lid and stir. You can set it to Manual or pressure cook at high pressure for one minute on Sealing mode.
3. After the cooking time is up, let the pressure go down on its own for 5 to 7 minutes. Then, slowly let go of the rest of the pressure so the sauce doesn't spray out of the pressure valve. When the pin hits the bottom, open the lid.
4. Start the Saute mode. Mix in the sugar. Cook the cranberry sauce for two to four minutes or until it starts to thicken and becomes like jam. As it cools, the sauce will keep getting thicker. Let it cool all the way down, then pour it into jars to store.

Instant Pot Chickpeas

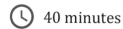 3 servings 🕐 40 minutes

Ingredients:

- 0.3 pound dried chickpeas
- 1.5 cups of cold water
- 1 tsp salt optional
- 0.3 clove garlic
- 0.15 medium yellow onion optional

Instructions:

1. Put your dried chickpeas through a mesh strainer and wash them well. Look through the chickpeas for any stones or broken ones and throw them away.
2. Chickpeas that have been dried up
3. With the beans, 5 cups of water, and any aromatics already in the pot, put them in after being rinsed.
4. 1.5 cups of cold water, 0.15 medium-sized yellow onions, 3 crushed garlic cloves, and 1 tsp of salt
5. Make sure the vent is set to "sealing" and the lid is sealed on the Instant Pot. Set the timer to 40 minutes or 45 minutes on Manual/High Pressure, depending on how firm or soft you want the chickpeas to be. For twenty minutes, it will get to that point.
6. After the pressure cooking cycle is over, let the pressure drop on its own for 15 to 20 minutes. Then, turn the vent to "venting" to let out the rest of the pressure.
7. Take off the lid and remove any scents. After cooking the chickpeas, strain them and use them however you like.

Instant Pot Sweet Potatoes

 3 servings 30 minutes

Ingredients:

- 0.38 cup of water
- 1.5 medium-sized sweet potatoes

Instructions:

1. Clean sweet potatoes and cut them into pieces if needed. Add water to the Instant Pot. Stick a wire rack at the bottom of the Instant Pot and put sweet potatoes on top of it.
2. Put the lid on and turn the valve to seal it.
3. Pick Up Pressure For 15 minutes, cook (or set the timer to high). It will get to pressure in ten minutes.
4. Do nothing for 15 minutes after the timer goes off to let the pressure go away on its own.
5. Let out the last bit of pressure, take off the lid, and serve.

Instant Pot Brussels Sprouts

 3 servings   🕐 5 minutes

Ingredients:

- 0.5 cup of water
- 0.5-pound brussels sprouts
- Salt and pepper

Instructions:

1. In the Instant Pot, add water and Brussels sprouts.
2. The Instant Pot's lid should be closed, and the valve should be turned to the Shut Off position.
3. Pick either "Manual" or "Pressure Cook" and set the timer for one minute.
4. Quickly release the steam when it's done cooking.
5. When the Brussels sprouts are done, drain them and add salt and pepper to taste.

Instant Pot Herb Roasted Potatoes

 3 servings   10 minutes

Ingredients:

- 0.38 cup of water
- 0.38 tsp dried marjoram
- 0.75 tsp kosher salt
- 2.25 tbsp olive oil
- 0.38 tsp dried rosemary
- 0.19 tsp pepper
- 0.38 tsp garlic powder
- 0.38 tsp dried oregano
- 0.38 tsp dried thyme
- 1.5 pounds baby Yukon golds and red potatoes

Instructions:

1. Dry the potatoes with a paper towel. Poke a hole in the middle of each potato with a fork.
2. Put oregano, marjoram, rosemary, thyme, garlic powder, salt, and pepper in a small bowl.
3. Press the Instant Pot's SAUTE button. When the screen says "HOT," add the oil and heat the Instant Pot with the lid off.
4. Add the potatoes one at a time and arrange them in a single layer.
5. Roll the potatoes around in the pan on all sides for a light brown and crisp finish. You could also fry the potatoes in a skillet over medium-low heat until they get a little brown, then move them to the Instant Pot.
6. Mix in the herb seasonings. Put in broth or water.
7. Ensure the sealing valve is set to SEALING, then close and lock the lid. For 7 minutes, press the button.
8. Press CANCEL and then turn the steam floating valve on the lid to the VENTING position to use QUICK RELEASE.
9. Take off the lid and put the potatoes on a platter to serve. Warm up and serve.

Instant Pot New Potatoes

 3 servings   13 minutes

Ingredients:

- 1.5 Tsp Butter
- 0.75 Tbsp Parsley
- Salt & Pepper
- 0.75 kg New Potatoes
- 0.75 Tbsp Extra Virgin Olive Oil
- 1.5 Tsp Garlic Puree

Instructions:

1. Put a cup of Water in the inner pot of your instant pot. Place your trivet on top of it and fill it with your new potatoes.
2. Put the lid on top of the instant pot and seal the valve. Cook on manual pressure for 8 minutes.
3. When it beeps, take the trivet off of the new potatoes and drain the Water from the bottom of the pot. Take the potatoes off the trivet and put them in a bowl.
4. Put the other ingredients in the bowl and mix them well.
5. Place the Crisplid trivet inside your instant pot and add the seasoned new potatoes.
6. Put the Mealthy Crisplid on top of the Instant Pot and cook at 220c/430f for 5 more minutes.
7. Serve while it's still warm.

Couscous & Vegetable Medley

 3 servings   20 minutes

Ingredients:

- 1 tsp Salt
- 1 Red Bell Pepper
- 1/2 Onion
- 1 3/4 cup of Couscous
- Cilantro to garnish
- 1 cup of Carrot
- 1 tbsp Lemon juice
- 2 Bay leaf
- 1 tbsp Olive Oil
- 2 cups of Water
- 1/2 tsp Garam masala

Instructions:

1. Add the Instant Pot on saute mode and add olive oil.
2. Put the onions and bay leaves in. Put it on for two minutes.
3. Carrots and bell peppers should be added. Cook for one more minute.
4. Salt, Water, and garam masala should all be added. Mix well.
5. Set the Instant Pot to "manual" for twice as long.
6. Do 10 minutes of NPR when the Instant Pot beeps. In other words, manually let go of the pressure 10 minutes after the beep.
7. It is time to fluff up the couscous; it is done. Add the lemon juice and stir. Add cilantro on top and serve hot.

Sweet Potato Casserole

Ingredients:

Pecan Topping:

- 0.25 tsp dried rosemary
- 1 tbsp maple syrup
- 0.5 cup of pecans coarsely

Casserole:

- 0.25 tsp pure vanilla extract
- 0.13 cup of whole milk
- Ground black pepper
- 0.5 tsp cinnamon
- 0.5 tbsp honey
- 0.38 tsp salt divided
- 0.25 cup of Water
- 1 tbsp butter or coconut oil
- 1 pound sweet potatoes

🍴 3 servings   🕐 20 minutes

Instructions:

1. In the Instant Pot, press "Saute" and wait for the screen to show "Hot." This should take about 4 to 5 minutes. Toast the pecans until they smell good, stirring every now and then (this will take about 7 minutes).
2. When you add the rosemary and 1 tbsp of maple syrup, stir it in well. Move to a bowl and press "Cancel" on the Instant Pot.
3. Put in the sweet potatoes, Water, and 1/4 tsp of salt. Things should not be wet on top of the potatoes. Bring the lid down, set the pressure valve to Sealing, and press the Pressure button. It should be set to High or Manual for 10 minutes.
4. Once the food is done, turn the pressure valve to the vent right away to let the pressure out. Make sure the sweet potatoes are really dry.
5. Mash the potatoes until they are smooth. Add the butter, milk, maple syrup, cinnamon, vanilla extract, 1/2 tsp of salt, and pepper.
6. Place the sweet potato mixture in an 8-by-8-inch square baking dish. Use a spatula to level it out, and then sprinkle the pecan topping on top.
7. You can put an egg to the mix and bake it without the topping for 20 minutes at 400 degrees F. We like it just the way it is. Then, put it on the top.

Creamy Garlic Broccoli Mash

 3 servings   🕐 5 minutes

Ingredients:

- 0.19 tsp black pepper
- 1.5 large cloves garlic
- 0.75-pound broccoli
- 3 ounce cream cheese
- 0.75 tbsp unsalted butter
- 0.38 cup of Water
- 0.19 tsp salt
- 0.19 tsp crushed red pepper flakes optional

Instructions:

1. Press "Saute" on the pressure cooker and wait two minutes for the pot to get hot. When the butter is almost gone, add the garlic. Cook for 30 seconds while stirring all the time. Just press "Cancel" to end the cooking.
2. Add the rest of the ingredients to the pot. Set the pot to Manual and High Pressure for one minute. After that, quickly let the pressure out.
3. To make the broccoli smoother, mash it with an immersion blender or a potato masher. You can taste it and put more salt and pepper if you want to.
4. Do it.

Instant Pot Cauliflower Rice

 3 servings   🕐 1 minutes

Ingredients:

- Juice of 1 lime
- 3 sprigs of cilantro
- 0.75 head of cauliflower
- 1.5 tbsp coconut oil

Instructions:

1. Take your cauliflower out of the package and wash it.
2. Then, cut the cauliflower into small pieces called florets.
3. The florets should be put on a silicone trivet, which should then be put in your instant pot.
4. After that, add one cup of Water to your Instant Pot.
5. Put the lid on top of your instant pot, and make sure the knob is all the way down.
6. Press the manual button hard, and set the timer for one minute.
7. To release the pressure, press "cancel" and use the quick pressure release method. The cauliflower will be cooked for one minute at high pressure.
8. Take the lid off the Instant Pot when all the pressure is gone.
9. Carefully take off the trivet that the cauliflower is on.
10. Take the stainless steel pot out of the Water and put it back in the instant pot.
11. Put extra virgin coconut oil in the pot. Set the Instant Pot to saute.
12. You can use a potato masher or a wooden spoon to mash the cauliflower until it looks like rice.
13. Put lime juice on the cauliflower. Give it a stir and wait one minute.
14. Take the cauliflower off the heat.
15. Add chopped cilantro on top.

Italian-Style Homemade Meatballs

Ingredients:

🍴 3 servings 🕐 7 minutes

For Meatballs:

- 0.38 pounds lean ground meat
- 0.38 large egg
- 0.75 tbsp fresh parsley
- 0.56 tsp salt
- 0.13 cup of panko breadcrumbs
- 0.28 tsp black pepper
- pinch red pepper flakes
- 0.09 cup of low-sodium beef broth
- 0.75 tbsp grated parmesan cheese
- 0.19 tbsp minced garlic

For Cooking Meatballs in a Pressure Cooker:

- 0.38 to 0.56 cup of beef broth

Instructions:

1. You should add 1 cup of Water or broth to the inner pot of a 3 or 6-quart pressure cooker. If you have an 8-quart pressure cooker, fill the inner pot with 1½ cups of Water or broth. Put a trivet or steamer basket inside the pot.
2. After putting the egg, bread crumbs, seasonings, and ¼ cup of beef broth in a large bowl, mix them together well. Mix in the ground meat until it's just mixed in. They will be tough if you mix them too much.
3. Roll the mixture into 1½-inch meatballs, using about 1 tbsp for each one. Put the trivet or steamer basket in the inner pot with the meatballs on top of it. It's fine if the meatballs need to be a little overlapping.
4. Put the lid on top of the pressure cooker and make sure the vent knob is set to "sealed" or the lid is locked. Use the manual or pressure cook button to set the timer for 5 minutes of high-pressure cooking.
5. Let the pressure drop on its own for at least 10 minutes before you try to do it yourself.
6. Add your favorite sauce to the meatballs and serve them.

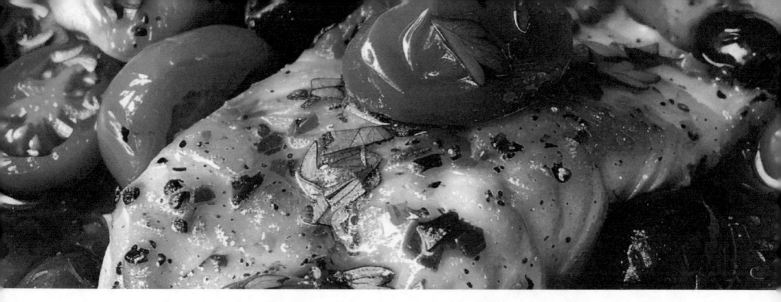

Instant Pot Fish Italian-Style

Ingredients:

🍴 3 servings 🕐 20 minutes

- A pinch of chili flakes
- 3 cloves garlic
- 9 cherry tomatoes
- 0.38 tsp salt
- 9-10.5 black olives
- 3 frozen white fish fillets
- 1.5 tbsp olive oil
- 0.19 cup of Water
- 0.25 cup of sliced roasted red peppers
- 1.5 tbsp marinated baby capers
- Garnish: chopped fresh parsley

Instructions:

1. Fill up the Instant Pot with Water. We only need ¼ cup because the frozen fish will give off a lot of liquid while it's cooking.
2. Put the fish fillets that have been frozen in the Water. Spread the rest of the ingredients out on top and around the food. Put some olive oil on top, and then add the sea salt and chili flakes.
3. Close and pop the lid. Press and hold the button. Turn the heat up to HIGH and cook for 4 minutes. The Instant Pot will start building up pressure, and cooking will begin after three beeps. Wait 7 to 8 minutes after the timer goes off for the pressure to release naturally. Then, do the quick release to get rid of the steam.
4. Carefully take out the fish fillets by opening the lid and using a spatula. The cooked food and broth should be poured over the top in that order. Put some chopped parsley or basil on top.

Russian Beef Rice Pilaf

Ingredients:

 3 servings   🕐 1 Hour

Instant Pot Beef Rice:
- 0.75-pound beef
- 0.75 cup of short-grain rice
- 0.75 cups of beef broth
- 1 tbsp oil
- 0.5 large onion
- 1 carrot
- 0.25 cup of tomato sauce

Instant Pot Plov Seasoning:
- 0.5 tsp garlic powder
- 0.25 tsp smoked paprika
- 0.5 head garlic
- 0.5 bay leaf
- 0.5 tsp black ground pepper
- 0.13 cup of chopped parsley
- 1 tsp salt
- 0.5 tsp beef seasoning

Instructions:

How to make Instant Pot Plov (One-Pot):

1. Set the Instant Pot to "Saute" (30 minutes). When the screen says "Hot," add 1 tbsp of oil and the 0.5-inch diced Onion. Cook for about 5 minutes or until the Onion turns a light golden color. Then add one Carrot cut into chunks and 0.75 pounds of beef cubes, and stir.
2. Next, add 0.5 tsp of ground pepper, 0.5 tsp of garlic powder, 0.25 tsp of smoked paprika, 0.5 tsp of beef seasoning (if using), 1 tsp of salt, 0.25 cup of tomato sauce, 0.5 bay leaf, 0.75 cups of beef stock. Stir.
3. Turn the steam valve to "sealing" and put a lid on top of the Instant Pot. Set the food processor to "Manual" and "High" for 45 minutes. After the time is up, put a kitchen towel over the steam valve and turn it to "venting" to let the pressure out. When the pressure goes down, open the lid.
4. Take the bay leaf off.
5. Spread the 1.5 cups of rice evenly with a spoon so that all the rice is covered with liquid. Do not stir the rice.
6. Press the cut side of the garlic head that has been cut in half into the rice. Set the steam valve to "sealing" and place the lid on top. Set the Instant Pot to "Manual" on "High" heat and begin the 15-minute timer.
7. When the time is up, turn off the Instant Pot and let it depressurize on its own for 15 to 20 minutes. This is an important step.
8. Next, change the steam valve to "venting" and let the rest of the steam go. Now, take off the lid, take out the garlic, and squeeze it back into the rice if you want. Add the parsley, and then use a fork to gently fluff the rice so that all ingredients are evenly spread.

Ethiopian Spicy Lentil Stew

🍴 3 servings   🕐 30 Minutes

Ingredients:

- 0.75 tsp fresh ginger
- 3 cloves garlic
- 1.5 to 2.25 cups of Water
- 0.75 medium red Onion
- 1.5 tbsp olive oil
- 0.75 tsp salt
- 0.38 lime
- 0.75 cup of split red lentils
- 0.75 to 2.25 tbsp berbere spice blend
- 1.5 tbsp cilantro

Instructions:

1. Set the Instant Pot to Saute. Add the onions and oil when the "hot" sign comes on. Combine well. Put a glass lid on top and cook for two minutes.
2. Put in garlic and ginger. In 30 seconds of cooking time, mix well.
3. Put in the salt, red lentils, and berbere spice blend. Mix everything together after adding 2 cups of Water.
4. Close the pressure valve on the Instant Pot lid to seal it. After 15 minutes of cooking on Manual (Hi), let the pressure release naturally.
5. Start up the Instant Pot and stir everything around. You can make the stew the consistency you want by adding more Water. Combine well.
6. Add chopped cilantro and fresh lime juice on top and serve with steamed rice or bread.

Mexican Instant Pot Beef Taco Meat

 3 servings   10 Minutes

Ingredients:

- ¼ cup of organic low-sodium beef broth
- taco seasoning 3 tbsp
- ⅓ to ⅗ pounds of lean ground beef
- ⅓ tbsp olive oil
- 4 ½ ounce cans of black beans

Instructions:

1. When the Instant Pot says "hot," press the "SAUTE" button and add the ground beef.
2. The beef is done when it's no longer pink. You can use a wooden spoon or a spatula to break it up. If you need to, drain the fat. Then add taco seasoning and mix it in.
3. Press "Cancel," and then add the beef broth. Put black beans on top of the beef. (if utilized) Pick up the pressure cooker, put the lid on top, and press "Pressure Cook" for 5 minutes.
4. It will take a few minutes for the pot to reach full pressure. After that, start the timer and cook for 5 minutes. Turn the vent knob for a quick release or do a manual release to keep the food warm until you serve it.
5. Take off the lid, stir the meat mixture, and serve when the pin falls. Press "SAUCE" to lower the amount of liquid, and cook for 5 minutes or until the liquid is gone.

Ukrainian Instant Pot Beet Soup

Ingredients:

🍴 3 servings   🕐 15 Minutes

- 0.19 white Cabbage medium head
- 1.5 beets medium
- 2.25 tbsp apple cider vinegar
- 1.5 tbsp olive oil
- 0.94 liters water
- 0.75 cube beef stock
- 0.75 onion medium white
- 0.75 pound white potatoes large
- 11.25 g dried porcini mushrooms
- 0.75 cube vegetable stock

- 3 cloves garlic medium cloves
- 0.75 tsp salt
- 0.75 carrot large
- 0.38 tsp pepper
- 1.13 tbsp tomato paste

To serve:
- 1.5 tbsp parsley fresh
- 3 tbsp sour cream optional

Instructions:

1. When you turn on the Instant Pot and press the Saute key, it should say "High, 30 minutes."
2. Put in the olive oil and onions. Cook for two minutes, until the onions get soft. Put in the beets, potatoes, and carrots and mix them in. Next, add the Cabbage, Garlic, and the rest of the ingredients. After you're done, press the "Keep Warm" or "Cancel" button.
3. Put the lid on and lock it. Make sure the handle that lets the steam out is pointing to Sealing. Set the timer for 10 minutes and press Manual (High Pressure). When you hear three beeps, the pressure cooker will move on. After the time is up, let the pressure drop on its own for 5 minutes. Then, use the quick release to get rid of the rest of the steam.
4. Put some chopped fresh parsley on top of the soup and top it with sour cream or full-fat Greek yogurt.

Instant Pot Korean Beef

Ingredients:

 3 servings   🕐 40 Minutes

- 0.75 tbsp freshly grated Ginger
- 0.19 tsp pepper
- 0.19 cup of reduced-sodium soy sauce
- 1.88 cloves minced garlic
- 0.19 tsp onion powder
- 0.09 cup of reduced-sodium beef broth
- 1.13-1.5 pound boneless beef chuck roast
- 0.75-1.5 tbsp Gochujang sauce
- 0.75 tbsp rice vinegar
- 0.13 cup of brown sugar packed
- 0.75 tbsp sesame oil

Instructions:

1. Gather the first 10 ingredients (up to roast) in a medium bowl and mix them with a whisk.
2. Put the cut-up roast into the Instant Pot.
3. Cover meat cubes with sauce.
4. Make sure the pressure release valve is set to "SEALING" and the lid is closed.
5. Set the timer for 40 minutes and press the MEAT program button. It should take about 10 to 15 minutes for the pot to reach pressure.
6. If the pot gets too hot, it will start counting down.
7. When it's done cooking, it will beep and turn to "keep warm."
8. You should let the beef stay in the pot for 25 minutes NPR—natural pressure release.
9. Turn the pressure release valve to "VENTING" to carefully let go of any remaining pressure.

Instant Pot Thai Chicken Curry

Ingredients:

 3 servings   🕐 20 Minutes

Part one:
- 3-3.75 slices of Ginger
- 0.75 medium onion
- 0.5 cup of chicken stock
- 0.75 tbsp fish sauce
- 1.05 pounds. Chicken breast
- 0.75 cup of coconut milk coconut cream
- 0.25 cup of red curry paste
- 1.5 garlic cloves
- 1.5 tsp sugar
- 0.75-1.5 tbsp olive oil

Part two:
- Juice of ½ lime
- 0.38 head of broccoli florets
- 0.38 large zucchini
- 0.75 red pepper
- 0.75 large Carrot s
- To thicken: 2 tbsp tapioca flour or arrowroot flour
- 0.19 cup of chopped Cilantro
- 0.19 cup of coconut cream
- Garnish: diced scallions/spring onions

Instructions:

1. When you turn on the Instant Pot, press the Saute button. Add Garlic, Ginger, Onion, and olive oil as soon as the pot is hot. Stir everything together. Stir the food for one minute, then add the chicken.
2. Mix the curry paste into the chicken. Add the chicken stock, fish sauce, sugar, and coconut cream now. Press "Cancel" to stop the Sauteing after giving it a good stir.
3. Place the lid on top and lock it. Make sure the valve points to Sealing. Press Manually or Firmly. Set the timer for 7 minutes on HIGH pressure and cook. The Instant Pot will say "ON," and the pressure will build up for 5 to 10 minutes. The timer will then begin. But the curry will be cooking the whole time.
4. After the timer goes off, let the pressure naturally drop for a few minutes. Then, use the quick-release method (turn the top valve to Venting) to let out the rest of the pressure. Watch out for the hot steam jet!
5. Press the Saute button again after opening the lid. Mix in half a lime juice. Try a little bit. If you want, you can add more salt or fish sauce.
6. Set the heat to Saute and add all the vegetables. Stir the food every now and then for three to four minutes.
7. Mix 2 tbsp of Water to the tapioca or arrowroot flour well. As you stir, the sauce will get thicker. Add the last bit of coconut cream, and then stir in the Cilantro.

Moroccan-Style Instant Pot Chickpea Stew

 3 servings   25 Minutes

Ingredients:

- 0.38 Tbsp. garlic
- 0.09 tsp. ground cinnamon
- 0.38 Tbsp. lemon juice
- 0.19 tsp. black pepper
- 0.38 cup of fennel large
- 0.19 tsp. ground turmeric
- 0.38 cup of yellow onions
- 0.09 tsp. Red pepper flakes
- 0.94 tsp. Sea salt

- 0.75 Tbsp. olive oil
- 0.38 cup of carrots diced
- 2.25 cups of vegetable broth
- 0.19 cup of celery diced
- 0.75 cups of sweet potatoes
- 11.25 ounce. Canned chickpeas
- 0.09 cup of maple syrup
- 0.38 tsp. ground cumin
- 0.09 tsp. ground coriander

Instructions:

1. For "saute," put oil, onions, ½ tsp of salt, and ½ tsp of black pepper in a pot that is off. Stirring often, cook for at least 5 minutes, but 10 minutes is better for slightly caramelized onions.
2. After you add the Garlic, cook and mix for another minute.
3. Add cumin, turmeric, coriander, cinnamon, red pepper flakes, and fennel for the spices. Then, mix everything together really well. The idea is to cover each vegetable with spices and let the spices toast a bit to make them more awake.
4. Last, add the rest of the salt, the broth, the lemon juice, the maple syrup, the sweet potatoes, the chickpeas, and the rest of the ingredients. Mix one last time. Put the lid back on and set the timer for 5 minutes. Quick-release the pressure when the cooking time is up.

Instant Pot Vegetable Lo Mein

🍴 3 servings   🕐 20 Minutes

Ingredients:

- 6 ounces Noodles
- ⅕ tsp Salt
- ⅕ tsp Black Pepper
- Sesame seeds

For the Sauce:
- ¾ tsp Brown sugar
- 1 ½ cups of Vegetable Broth
- ¾-1 ½ tsp Red chili paste
- ¾ tsp Ginger
- 1 ½ tsp Sesame oil

- 2 ¼ tbsp Soy Sauce
- ¾ tsp Garlic
- ¾ tbsp Vinegar

Vegetables:
- ⅜ cup of Bell Pepper
- ⅜ cup of Cabbaged
- ⅜ cup of Broccoli
- ⅕ cup of Scallion
- ¾ Carrot

Instructions:

1. Put everything you need for the sauce in a bowl. Whisk until everything is well mixed. Test and make changes as needed.
2. Break up the spaghetti and add it to the Instant Pot.
3. Add the sauce above to the pot where the noodles are. On top, put all the vegetables except the Broccoli.
4. Put the lid on your Instant Pot and set it to "manual" for 4 minutes at high pressure.
5. Quickly let the pressure out of the Instant Pot when it's done cooking.
6. Take off the lid and add the broccoli florets. Be sure they are broken up into little pieces. With tongs, stir the noodles several times to break up any that may have clumped together while they were cooking. To taste, add salt and black pepper. For 5 minutes, close the lid and let the broccoli cook. Do not pressure cook at this point.
7. Take off the lid. Put sesame seeds and green onions on top, and serve.

VEGETARIAN AND VEGAN

Instant Pot Carrots

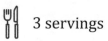 3 servings    12 Minutes

Ingredients:

- 1.5-pound carrots
- 1.5 cup of Water
- fresh herbs
- salt and pepper
- 1.5 tbsp extra-virgin olive oil

Instructions:

1. Get the carrots clean and peel them. Cut the ends off and then cut across the grain.
2. Put the carrots in the Instant Pot and add Water.
3. Put the handle on "sealing" and the lid on top of the Instant Pot. Cook on high pressure for two minutes. Once it's done, quickly let the steam out carefully, take off the lid, and drain the carrots.
4. Put the carrots in a different bowl and put the extra-virgin olive oil, salt, pepper, and fresh herbs, if you want to use them. Serve and Enjoy.

Instant Pot Lentils & Rice

 3 servings   30 Minutes

Ingredients:

- ⅜ cup of Brown lentils
- ⅜ cup of Basmati Rice
- ¼ tbsp Garlic
- 1 cup of Water for cooking
- ¼ Onion
- ¼ Onion
- 1 tbsp Oil to saute onions

- ⅛ cup of Cilantro
- Spices:
- ⅛ tsp Ground Cinnamon
- ½ tsp Ground Coriander
- ½ tsp Salt
- ¼ tsp Ground Cumin

Instructions:

1. Rinse the brown lentils and put them in warm Water for an hour.
2. Add the Instant Pot on saute mode and add 1 tbsp of oil. The onions should be sauteed for about 5 minutes until they turn brown and get a little crispy around the edges. Get them out and put them away for now.
3. Put one tbsp of oil in the instant pot. Add the Garlic and onions that have been cut up. For about 3 minutes, cook them until they get a light brown color. You can now add the salt, cumin, cinnamon, and ground coriander.
4. Add the lentils and Water and mix them in. For about six to seven minutes, let it boil. Before we add the rice, this will help the lentils get softer.
5. Mix the rice well after adding it. Press "cancel," then close the lid with the vent in the "sealing" position.
6. Use the Rice mode to cook. The Instant Pot set the timer for 12 minutes of low-pressure cooking. Let the pressure drop on its own for 10 minutes, and then release it by hand. Stop the instant pot and take the steel insert out.
7. Use a fork to fluff up the rice and lentils. Add the sliced onions that have been caramelized and the Cilantro on top of the rice. Serve with yogurt and salad.

Instant Pot Lemon Vegetable Risotto

 3 servings  27 Minutes

Ingredients:

- 1.5 tbsp lemon juice
- 0.75 tsp fresh thyme
- 0.75 tsp lemon zest
- 0.38 tsp garlic powder
- 0.75 cup of fresh peas
- 0.75-0.38 cups of arborio rice
- 0.75 cup of broccoli florets
- 0.38 bunch of chives

- 0.75 onion
- 3 cups of vegetable broth
- 1.5 garlic cloves
- 3 tbsp butter
- 0.75 cup of leek diced
- 1.5 tbsp and 1 tsp extra-virgin olive oil
- 0.19 tsp red pepper flakes
- 0.75 cup of spinach

Instructions:

1. Warm the oven up to 400 °F. Add parchment paper on the bottom of a baking sheet. Corn, Broccoli, and peas should all be put on the baking sheet. Add pepper, salt, and one tsp of extra-virgin olive oil. Toss the food well. Broccoli should be soft enough to pierce with a fork after 15 to 20 minutes in the oven. Take it out of the oven and set it aside when it's done.
2. If you have an Instant Pot or other pressure cooker, press SAUTE. Adding the last bit of extra-virgin olive oil and waiting for it to warm up. Add the Garlic, onions, and leeks once the oil is hot. Wait two to three minutes or until the onions become clear.
3. To toast the rice, add it and stir for one to two minutes.
4. Put in the butter, thyme, and vegetable stock. Mix well.
5. The pressure cooker or instant pot needs to be turned off. Put the lid back on, turn the valve to Sealing, press "manual," and change the time to 7 minutes.
6. The pressure cooker is done when the timer goes off. To quickly let the pressure out, turn the valve to the vent. Take off the lid and stir it around a lot.
7. Change the setting to SAUTE. Add chives, roasted vegetables, spices, and lemon juice to the rice. When the spinach starts to wilt, stir it for one to two minutes. Add more salt or pepper if you like. Add more chives and lemon zest on top.

Instant Pot Vegan Congee

Ingredients:

 3 servings   30 Minutes

- 1.5-2.25 Ginger
- 0.75 cup of Jasmine Rice
- 4.5 cups of Water
- 1.5 tsp Vegetable Bouillon omit
- 0.75 tbsp Kosher Salt
- 1.5-2.25 cloves Garlic

Toppings:
- 0.75 tsp Shredded pickled Ginger
- 0.38 cup of Shiitake Mushrooms
- 0.19 cup of Sliced scallions
- 1.5 cloves Garlic
- 0.38 tsp Chili-Garlic oil
- 0.38 tsp Sesame seeds

Instructions:

1. Rinse the rice briefly in a small bowl to get rid of most of the starch. Some starch is good for this, so you don't have to rinse it as well as you would for regular rice.
2. Add the bouillon to the warm Water that you need to cook the rice. Only needs to be done if not using regular vegetable broth.
3. Cut and peel 2-3 big pieces of Ginger and three garlic cloves that have been smashed.
4. Put the rice that has been rinsed and the broth in the instant pot.
5. Add the salt, Ginger, and Garlic and mix them in.
6. Place the lid on top and seal the valve. Cook on HIGH pressure for 30 minutes.
7. Let the congee loosen up on its own until the pin falls. It could take 30 minutes or more.
8. Get the toppings ready while the congee is cooking.
9. To make the mushrooms, slice the shiitake mushrooms and cook them in butter or oil until they get soft. Add a little salt to taste.
10. For the fried Garlic, slice it very thinly. Cut 2 to 3 garlic cloves in half lengthwise. Warm oil up in a pot or pan that isn't deep. Slice the Garlic and add it to the hot oil. Cook it all the way through until it turns golden brown. Watch out not to burn.
11. Cut up green onions.
12. Take the lid off the instant pot once the congee is done, and the pressure has gone down on its own.
13. To keep the congee from sticking and to help the steam escape, stir it around a few times.
14. Use a spoon or fork to take the garlic cloves and pieces of Ginger out of the instant pot.
15. Place bowls of congee on a plate. Add fried Garlic, mushrooms in oil, pickled Ginger, sliced green onions, Cilantro, chili garlic oil, and sesame seeds (or any other toppings you like).
16. Use a spoon to eat it!

Instant Pot Vegetarian Chili with Quinoa

 3 servings   25 Minutes

Ingredients:

- 1 ½ cups of Vegetable Broth
- 2 ¼ cloves Garlic
- 4/7 tbsp Chili powder
- ⅜ tbsp Paprika
- ¾ tsp Salt
- ¾ cup of Corn
- ¾ can Black beans
- ¾ cup of Yellow Onion
- ¾ can Fire-roasted diced Tomatoes
- ¼ cup of Quinoa
- ⅜ Jalapeno

- ¾ tsp Ground Cumin
- ¾ cup of Green Bell Pepper

Optional Toppings:
- Red Onion
- Sour cream
- Cilantro leaves
- Jalapeno
- Tortilla chips
- Lemon wedges
- Avocado
- Cheddar Cheese

Instructions:

1. Put all ingredients into your Instant Pot in the order given.
2. Close the lid with the vent in the closed position. For 6 minutes at high pressure, set the machine to pressure cook mode.
3. When the pressure cooker beeps, let the pressure drop on its own. Take off the lid. If the salt is too high, add more. Add cilantro leaves as a garnish.
4. Add any of the toppings you want and serve!

Made in United States
Cleveland, OH
20 February 2025

14451805R00044